Zen in the Stable

Wisdom from the Equestrian Life

LAINE CUNNINGHAM

Zen in the Stable
Wisdom from the Equestrian Life

Published by Sun Dogs Creations
Changing the World One Book at a Time
Softcover ISBN: 9781946732125
Hardcover ISBN: 9781946732132

Softcover Edition

Cover Design by Angel Leya

Copyright © 2017 and 2019 Laine Cunningham

All rights reserved. No part of this book may be reproduced in any form or by any means, electronic, mechanical, digital, photocopying or recording, except for the inclusion in a review, without permission in writing from the publisher.

Introduction

From an early age, I was obsessed with horses. Their power and grace demonstrated the natural ease with which we can move through our lives. Their fluid movements promised to carry me into new worlds, ones that could only be viewed from horseback.

Around the time I turned fifteen, my parents met a young couple who had transferred to our military base. The wife was a lifelong equestrian who had been offered a slot on the Olympic team. Although she had decided to attend college instead, she was not ready to give up riding.

Under her expert guidance, I took up English riding, dressage and jumping. Soon we were competing in local events. I learned that working with horses is spiritual. The rider must be calm and collected while honoring their partner.

Equestrian activity demands deep connection. When that happens, horse and rider transcend. *Zen in the Stable* honors that relationship.

Longeing winds the clock of meditation.

Few riders will reach the Olympics. Few riders need to.

Hoofbeats mirror the heartbeat.

A single paddock contains the world.

An extended gait enables thrust and reach.

Oats are a nutrient and a reward.

Dressage emulates natural grace.

The scent of hay is sweeter than nectar.

Trail rides broaden your perspective.

Properly maintained tack supports the best performance.

Adjust the stride to suit the course.

The stone that hinders yields to a pick.

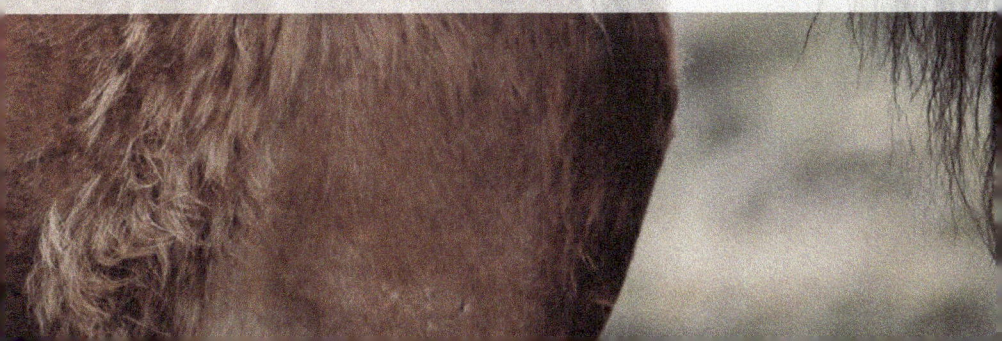
A soft muzzle heals the wounded heart.

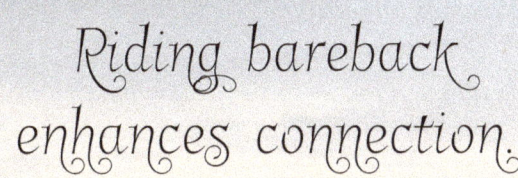

Riding bareback enhances connection.

The horse is not equal to the rider.
Nor is the rider equal to the horse.

A straight horse develops symmetrically.

The turnout of a dressage horse does not affect the score.

The ribbon topping the tail cannot disguise the danger.

A warm barn shelters the soul.

Soft hands encourage contact.

Freestyle riding demands trust.

A shared stable creates a community.

Competitiveness should be corralled inside the ring.

A half pass travels beyond rather than through.

A supple horse bends easily under saddle.

Relaxation allows for smooth transitions.

Mucking out stalls enhances spiritual growth.

Foam on the withers marks your zest for life.

Hind legs that follow the front channel power to the center.

Master the flying change to manage the corners.

Every horse knows at least one trick.

Pirouette at different degrees to meet different goals.

Equestrian passion demands impassioned effort.

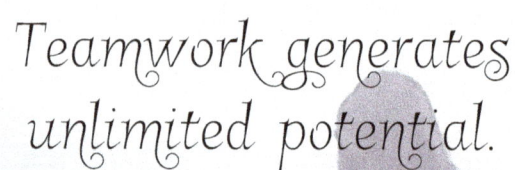

Teamwork generates unlimited potential.

Airs above the ground generate flight.

Hunters require calmness and style.

A collected gait adjusts the stride.

Manure nurtures a verdant pasture.

The fanciest outfit does not a hunter make.

A well-shod horse has a sturdy foundation.

The rider must balance with the horse.

A ragged mane can be beautifully plaited.

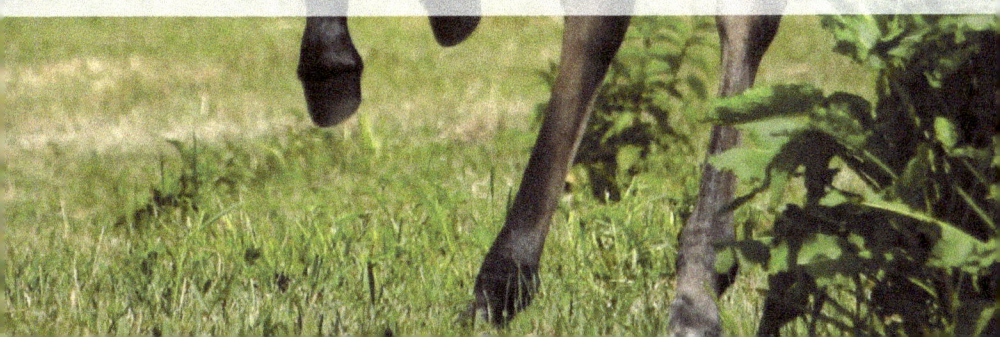
Jumpers require boldness and control.

Horses of unknown parentage have become champions.

A still trough offers a true reflection.

About the Author

Laine Cunningham's books take readers on adventures around the world. *The Family Made of Dust* is set in the Australian Outback, while *Reparation* is a novel of the American Great Plains. Her women's travel adventure memoir *Woman Alone: A Six-Month Journey Through the Australian Outback* appeals to fans of *Wild* and *Eat Pray Love*. Her work has received multiple awards including the Hackney and the James Jones Fellowship, and has been published by *Reed*, *Birmingham Arts Journal*, and the annual anthology by *Writer's Digest*. She is the senior editor of *Sunspot Literary Journal*.

Fiction

The Family Made of Dust
Beloved
Reparation

Nonfiction

Woman Alone

On the Wallaby Track: Australian Words and Phrases

Seven Sisters: Messages from Aboriginal Australia

Writing While Female or Black or Gay

The Wisdom of Puppies
The Wisdom of Babies
The Wisdom of Weddings

The Zen of Travel
The Zen of Gardening
Zen in the Stable
The Zen of Chocolate
The Zen of Dogs

Bikes of Berlin
Necropolises of New Orleans I & II
Ruins of Rome I & II
Ancients of Assisi I & II
Panoramas of Portugal
Nuances of New York
Glimpses of Germany
Impressions of Italy
Altitudes of the Alps
Knights Through the Ages
Utopia of the Unicorn
Portraits of Paris
Flourishes of France

www.ingramcontent.com/pod-product-compliance
Lightning Source LLC
Chambersburg PA
CBHW041959080526
44588CB00021B/2808